Spring Harvest
Bible Workbook

DAVID

After God's Own Heart

LIFESTYLE

SPRING HARVEST

Equipping the Church for action

First published in 2003 Spring Harvest Publishing Division and Authentic Lifestyle

09 08 07 06 05 04 03   7 6 5 4 3 2 1

Authentic Lifestyle is an imprint of Authentic Media

PO Box 300, Carlisle, Cumbria, CA3 0QS, UK

and Box 1047, Waynesboro, GA 30830-2047, USA

www.paternoster-publishing.com

British Library Cataloguing in Publication Data

A catalogue record for this book is available from the British Library

ISBN 1-85078-497-3

Typeset by Spring Harvest
Cover design by Diane Bainbridge
Printed in Great Britain by Bell and Bain Ltd., Glasgow

CONTENTS

ABOUT THIS BOOK

This book is written primarily for a group situation, but can easily be read by individuals who want to study the life of David. It can be used in a variety of contexts, so it is perhaps helpful to spell out the assumptions that we have made about the groups that will use it. These can have a variety of names – homegroups, Bible study groups, cell groups – we've used housegroup as the generic term.

▶ The emphasis of the studies will be on the application of the Bible. Group members will not just learn facts, but will be encouraged to think 'How does this apply to me? What change does it require of me? What incidents or situations in my life is this relevant to?'

▶ Housegroups can encourage honesty and make space for questions and doubts. The aim of the studies is not to find the right answer but to help members understand the Bible by working through their questions. The Christian faith throws up paradoxes. Events in people's lives can make particular verses difficult to understand. The housegroup should be a safe place to express these concerns.

▶ Housegroups can give opportunities for deep friendships to develop. Group members will be encouraged to talk about their experiences, feelings, questions, hopes and fears. They will be able to offer one another pastoral support and get involved in each other's lives.

▶ There is a difference between being a collection of individuals who happen to meet together every Wednesday and being an effective group who bounce ideas off each other, spark inspiration and creativity, pooling their talents and resources to create solutions together: one whose whole is definitely greater than the sum of its parts. The process of working through these studies will encourage healthy group dynamics.

Space is given for you to write answers, comments, questions and thoughts. This book will not tell you what to think, but will help you discover the truth of God's word through thinking, discussing, praying and listening.

FOR GROUP MEMBERS

▶ You will probably get more out of the study if you spend some time during the week reading the passage and thinking about the questions. Make a note of anything you don't understand.

▶ Pray that God will help you to understand the passage and show you how to apply it. Pray for other members in the group, too, that they will find the study helpful.

▶ Be willing to take part in the discussions. The leader of the group is not there as an expert with all the answers. They will want everyone to get involved and share their thoughts and opinions.

▶ However, don't dominate the group! If you are aware that you are saying a lot, make space for others to contribute. Be sensitive to other group members and aim to be encouraging. If you disagree with someone, say so but without putting down their contribution.

FOR INDIVIDUALS

▶ Although this book is written with a group in mind, it can also easily be used by individuals. You obviously won't be able to do the group activities suggested, but you can consider how you would answer the questions and write your thoughts in the space provided.

▶ You may find it helpful to talk to a prayer partner about what you have learnt, and ask them to pray for you as you try and apply what you are learning to your life.

▶ The New International Version of the text is printed in the book. If you use a different version, then read from your own Bible as well.

This workbook draws on material from Ian Coffey's book *The Story of David*, published by Spring Harvest. You'll find it excellent background reading with fresh insight into many episodes from David's life.

Other titles in this Spring Harvest Bible Studies series:

Sermon on the Mount – ISBN 1-85078-407-8
Based on the Spring Harvest 2000 theme, King of the Hill.

Jesus at the Centre – ISBN 1-85078-440-X
Based on the Spring Harvest 2001 theme, A Royal Banquet.

Letters to the Churches – ISBN 1-85078-441-8
Based on the Spring Harvest 2002 theme, You've Got Mail.

Big Themes from Colossians – ISBN 1-85078-457-4
Based on the Spring Harvest 1999 theme, Across the Borderline.

Mission of God – ISBN 1-85078-496-5
Based on the Spring Harvest 2003 theme, Shepherd's Bush to King's Cross.

Jonah – God's Compassion – ISBN 1-85078-508-2
Studies on Jonah.

Moses – Friend of God – ISBN 1-85078-519-8
Studies on Moses.

Connect! Workbook – ISBN 1-85078-521-X
Based on Tim Jeffery and Steve Chalke's ground-breaking book rethinking mission for the 21st century.

INTRODUCTION TO DAVID
A MAN AFTER GOD'S OWN HEART

Surely someone described as 'a man after God's own heart' should be a paragon of virtue, an icon for us to imitate?

And yet in David, like all the Old Testament fathers, we find a flawed hero.

Yes, he killed Goliath; waited patiently for God to establish him on the throne; drew strength from God; was a model friend to Jonathan and, much of the time, was a wise king. But David also knew what it was like to give into temptation and to fail. His adulterous affair with Bathsheba, the murder of her husband and his dismal efforts to preserve family unity were not his greatest moments.

David knew the extremes of human existence – he had enjoyed the best of friendships but endured the bitterest of betrayals when his son and closest advisor conspired to take away his throne. He knew what it was like to live like an animal in the caves and what it was to enjoy luxurious opulence in a magnificent palace.

But despite his personal failings and this mixture of life experiences, the fact remains that God chose to promote this shepherd boy to be the shepherd of his people. God determined that from his line would come the Saviour of the world.

So why did David deserve the epitaph 'A man after God's own heart'? What was it that pleased God when he looked at David? Perhaps it was David's overwhelming desire for intimacy with God. He never tried to rob God of power but saw the divine handprint over all of his life and responded with a sensitive, generous heart. Perhaps what pleased God most of all was that David knew how to repent.

The life of David challenges and inspires us but, more than that, it offers us hope; that we too can know a life-satisfying intimacy with God. We hope that, despite our failings, we too can be men and women 'after God's own heart'.

GOD'S CHOICE

 AIM: Learning to discern and live out God's will

The only memory I have of my first trip to London is going to the ice cream parlour 'Baskin and Robbins'. I remember, as a child, being lifted up and dangled over all the mouth-watering flavours until I finally chose one – vanilla! I was frightened I wouldn't like any of the others! Many of us find it difficult to make choices, especially if we're trying to discern God's will in a particular matter. And at times, learning to live with the consequences of these decisions can be even harder.

The Lord said to Samuel, 'How long will you mourn for Saul, since I have rejected him as king over Israel? Fill your horn with oil and be on your way; I am sending you to Jesse of Bethlehem. I have chosen one of his sons to be king. You are to anoint for me the one I indicate.'

When they arrived, Samuel saw Elihab and thought, 'Surely the Lord's anointed stands here before the Lord.'

But the Lord said to Samuel, 'Do not consider his appearance or his height, for I have rejected him. The Lord does not look at the things man looks at. Man looks at the outward appearance, but the Lord looks at the heart.'

Then Jesse called Abinadab and had him pass in front of Samuel. But Samuel said, 'The Lord has not chosen this one either.' Jesse then made Shammah pass by, but Samuel said, 'Nor has the Lord chosen this one.' Jesse made seven of his sons pass before Samuel, but Samuel said to him, 'The Lord has not chosen these.' So he asked Jesse, 'Are these all the sons you have?'

'There is still the youngest,' Jesse answered, 'but he is tending the sheep.'

Samuel said, 'Send for him; we will not sit down until he arrives.'

So he sent and had him brought in. He was ruddy, with a fine appearance and handsome features.

Then the Lord said, 'Rise and anoint him; he is the one.'

So Samuel took the horn of oil and anointed him in the presence of his brothers, and from that day on the Spirit of the Lord came upon David in power. Samuel then went to Ramah.

1 Samuel 16:1,3, 6-13

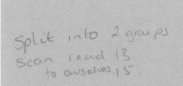

TO SET THE SCENE
Share together times when you've had to make important decisions. How did you know what decision to take? How were you able to discern what God's will was for your situation?

BACKGROUND
1   What do you know about Samuel?

2 What had Saul done to be rejected by God as Israel's king?
Scan 1 Samuel 13 and 15.

3 Although it was Saul's own actions and attitudes that led to his downfall, there were signs of trouble from before his reign. What were they? Look at 1 Samuel 8 for the way in which the Israelites approached the whole issue of asking God for a king.

Read 1 Samuel 16:1-13

4   God has already rejected Saul as king and had David in mind as a replacement (1 Sam. 16:1). Why was Samuel slow to recognise this? Why are we often slow to discern God's will?

5 We are not told in 16:3 how God would point David out to Samuel. What pointers do you think we should look for when we're trying to discern God's will?

[handwritten note:] Split into 2 groups
Scan read 13
to ourselves, 15

APPLY THIS TO

MY CHURCH

6 Seeing people and situations through God's eyes is a life lesson.

   a) In your church context, what type of labels do you tend to give people?
   b) How can we avoid this habit and view people as God does?

It takes but a moment to make a convert;
it takes a lifetime to manufacture a saint.
Alan Redpath

HOW DOES THIS

APPLY TO ME

7 Imagine God looking at the various categories of your life:

▶ Family
▶ Church
▶ Work
▶ Society

What would he think of the choices you've made in these areas? What elements would he give a higher priority to? What changes can you make to share his concerns?

8 God's will for David's life didn't just start when he finally became king, twenty years later. This preparation time was all part of God's plan for the man that David would become. What lessons do you think David needed to learn before he became king?

David at thirty-seven was more than he was at seventeen – more praise, saner counsel, deeper love. More himself. More his God-given and God-glorifying humanity. A longer stride, a larger embrace.
Eugene Peterson

9   Maybe you can identify with David – God's will for your life now means trusting him while you wait for him to act. Perhaps you're waiting for a child to come back to the Lord or a relationship to be restored. Pray together in twos that God would graciously intervene.

WORSHIP

For many people, God's will is difficult to live with. It may involve hardship, waiting or separation from family. Whatever your situation, be determined to worship God. Read David's Psalm 19 together and use it to inspire prayers and songs of praise to God. If it's appropriate, pray for those with specific difficulties or those seeking God's will in a particular matter.

FOR NEXT WEEK

Focus on seeing people and situations with God's eyes. How does this change your reactions and perceptions?

TRUE FRIENDSHIPS

AIM: To recognise the value of friendships on our spiritual journey

Do you remember the old saying 'You become like the people you spend time with'? It's true, isn't it? You can tell a lot about a person from their friends. Depending on which friends we choose, they can either shape us positively or negatively. What influence are your friends having on you?

> *After David had finished talking with Saul, Jonathan became one in spirit with David, and he loved him as himself. From that day Saul kept David with him and did not let him return to his father's house. And Jonathan made a covenant with David because he loved him as himself. Jonathan took off the robe he was wearing and gave it to David, along with his tunic, and even his sword, his bow and his belt.*

1 Samuel 18:1-4

TO SET THE SCENE

Share with each other about your 'best friends'. Talk about friendships from the past or about an individual whom you're friendly with now. What made this person your best friend? What are some of the special times together you remember?

1　Divide into two groups; one group all female, the other all male. Brainstorm what friendship looks like for your particular gender. What are the traits of male/female friendship? If appropriate, talk about any things that make it hard for you to make friends. Share your answers with the whole group.

WHAT DOES
SEARCH
THE BIBLE SAY?

2　Break up into small groups and scan some of the following references. How did David demonstrate his friendship to Jonathan and vice versa?

▶　Samuel 19:1–7
▶　Samuel 20
▶ 2 Samuel 1:23–27
▶ 2 Samuel 9

Read 1 Samuel 18:1–4

3　What was the significance of Jonathan's actions in 1 Samuel 18:1–4?

4　Given that Jonathan was also a proficient soldier (1 Sam. 14:4–14) how could his relationship with David have been a negative one? Look at 1 Samuel 18:5–9.

HOW DOES THIS
APPLY TO ME

5　In his book, Ian Coffey lists the qualities that David and Jonathan demonstrated in their friendship. Look at the list below and use it to measure your own relational skills. Which areas do you need to improve?

▶　Commitment
▶　Putting others first
▶　Risk
▶　Acts of kindness
▶　Protection
▶　Thinking and speaking well of others
▶　Long term investment
▶　Loving people when they are absent as much as when they are present
▶　Not being afraid to show true feelings

6 Read 1 Samuel 23:15-18 – this records the final meeting of the two friends. Jonathan helped David 'find strength in God'. How do you think he would have done this?

HOW DOES THIS **7** Do you have a David/Jonathan type friendship with someone? Is there someone who you could be a Jonathan to, someone APPLY TO ME you could help 'find strength in God'?

WHAT DOES **8** What makes people friends of God? SEARCH Look at Exodus 33:11, James 2:23, John 15:9-17. THE BIBLE SAY?

HOW DOES THIS **9** Using the criteria you discussed from question 8, how would you rate your friendship with God? Use the scale of 1-10, APPLY TO ME with 1 being poor and 10 excellent. What could you do to improve your relationship with God?

WORSHIP

Jesus said 'I no longer call you servants, because a servant does not know his master's business. Instead I have called you friends' (Jn. 15:15). Thank Jesus for the specific ways he has demonstrated his friendship to us. Use the traits in question 5 as a starting point. Then give time for reflection, as individuals quietly make their commitment to God to improve their friendship with him.

FOR NEXT WEEK

It is easy to take friends for granted, so do something special for your friend this week. Take them out for coffee, have an evening out together, give them a small gift – just some act of kindness to show you care.

ACTIVITY PAGE

For many of us, the problem is not how to improve our friendships with other Christians but how to begin to build relationships with non-Christians. Consider the following scenarios and decide what you would advise:

▶ A young Christian couple only come to the Sunday morning service because they go out with their non-Christian friends at night. They say it is the only night of the week they are able to do this. They see what they are doing as friendship evangelism but others in the church feel it reflects a lack of commitment and sets a bad example. What do you think?

▶ Your office is having a Christmas party. You know people will get drunk and there'll be things going on that you won't feel comfortable with. Should you go to show them Christians aren't boring and use it to develop relationships with your colleagues or should you stay away because it's not your scene?

▶ You always feel guilt-ridden when there is a guest service or special event at church because you don't feel you have any non-Christian friends to invite. Work is so busy and you barely have time to nod to the other parents when you pick up the children from school. What could you do to develop friendships with non-Christians?

LIVING WITH THE ENEMY

AIM: To learn how to deal with opposition to our faith

Jesus said 'Love your enemies, do good to those who hate you' (Lk. 6:27). But as enemies of the Christian faith increase on the world scene and in our own personal situations, what does it mean to love them? How do we love those who so vehemently oppose us? How do we practically show them love without appearing to condone their actions?

> *Saul was told that David had gone to Keilah, and he said, 'God has handed him over to me, for David has imprisoned himself by entering a town with gates and bars.' And Saul called up all his forces for battle, to go down to Keilah to besiege David and his men.*
>
> *When David learned that Saul was plotting against him, he said to Abithar the priest, 'Bring the ephod.' David said 'O Lord, God of Israel, your servant has heard definitely that Saul plans to come to Keilah and destroy the town on account of me. Will the citizens of Keilah surrender me to him? Will Saul come down, as your servant has heard? O Lord, God of Israel, tell your servant.'*
>
> *And the Lord said, 'He will.'*
>
> *Again David asked, 'Will the citizens of Keilah surrender me and my men to Saul?'*
>
> *And the Lord said, 'They will.'*
>
> *So David and his men, about six hundred in number, left Keilah and kept moving from place to place. When Saul was told that David had escaped from Keilah, he did not go there.*
>
> *David stayed in the desert strongholds and in the hills of the Desert of Ziph. Day after day Saul searched for him, but God did not give David into his hands.*
>
> **1 Samuel 23:7-14**

TO SET THE SCENE

Give each person a newspaper to look through. Find examples of people, institutions, lifestyles and beliefs that are opposing Christianity today. Discuss your findings together.

Read 1 Samuel 23:7-14

1 Initially David enjoyed the king's favour. He'd killed Goliath and was the court musician. So why, according to 1 Samuel 18:5-16, did Saul grow to hate David so much? Pick out as many reasons as you can.

2 Scan through 1 Samuel 18-20. How many times did Saul try to kill David?

WHAT DOES
SEARCH
THE BIBLE SAY?

3 David describes being surrounded by his enemies in his prayer journal – the Book of Psalms. Divide into two groups, with one group looking at Psalm 23, the other at Psalm 59. Given his life as a fugitive, does anything surprise you about David's attitude and beliefs?

4 On two occasions David had the opportunity to kill Saul but he refused. Why? Look at 1 Samuel 24: 5-7,15; 26:5-25.

HOW DOES THIS
APPLY TO ME

5 What lessons do David's actions and attitudes towards Saul teach us about how to deal with our enemies?

HOW DOES THIS
APPLY TO ME

6 How can we avoid becoming like Saul – bitter and jealous of others, someone who quenches God's spirit?

7 David faced Goliath, the enemy from the opposing army. Now Saul, a fellow Israelite and father of his best friend, is out to get him. In the same way, we often face opposition from within the Christian community and from without. Which do you find most difficult to cope with and why?

WHAT DOES SEARCH THE BIBLE SAY?

8 What good, if any, can dealing with enemies do for our spiritual development? Look back to the life of David and at Acts 14:22, 1 Peter 1:6-7; 4:16-19 for ideas.

WORSHIP

We each have our own enemies to face. On a piece of paper, write down your own particular enemy – the difficulty you're facing, the person or circumstance that is testing your Christian faith. Fold the paper up and with a drawing pin or nail, fix it to the notice board. As you do this, remember that when Jesus was nailed to the cross, he defeated the enemy once and for all. Thank him for his victory and then spend time in twos, asking for God's grace and wisdom to cope with your particular situations.

FOR NEXT WEEK

We often get accustomed to having enemies instead of trying to resolve our difficulties. As far as it is up to you, be like David and try to make peace with those who oppose you this week.

ACTIVITY PAGE

Remember those in prison as if you were their fellow prisoners, and those who are mistreated as if you yourselves were suffering.

Hebrews 13:3

Christians around the world face many enemies. Some face institutional enemies when the regime or state religion of their country is opposed to Christianity. The writer of Hebrews urges us to pray for these believers with the same urgency and intensity we would have if we were in their situation.

Think of ways you could pray more regularly for the persecuted church. Here are some ideas:

▶ Start prayer groups in your church for particular countries – use Patrick Johnstone's book Operation World as a resource
▶ Organise a special evening based around a particular country
▶ Try making their national dish
▶ Learn a national song
▶ Pray for the country using information from the internet or *Operation World*
▶ Contact a mission agency for names and needs of missionaries you could pray for
▶ Write to the missionary asking how you could help them practically
▶ Other organisations you could contact for information – Tearfund, Open Doors
▶ Organise a special Sunday where you can pray for the persecuted church. Get information from various mission organisations so that you can pray for a number of countries and the up-to-date needs of the Christians who live there.

MAINTAINING YOUR FOCUS

AIM: Learning how to keep God as the focus of our attention

What makes a great leader? What made Napoleon or Winston Churchill great? For a start, they both had tremendous determination and focus in the midst of adversity. At the biggest crisis point of his life so far, with his village in the Philistine territory devastated by the enemy and his own soldiers about to mutiny, what type of leader would David prove to be?

David and his men reached Ziklag on the third day. Now the Amalekites had raided the Negev and Ziklag. They had attacked Ziklag and burned it, and had taken captive the women and all who were in it, both young and old. They killed none of them, but carried them off as they went on their way.

When David and his men came to Ziklag, they found it destroyed by fire and their wives and sons and daughters taken captive. So David and his men wept aloud until they had no strength left to weep. David's two wives had been captured – Ahinoam of Jezreel and Abigail, the widow of Nabal of Carmel. David was greatly distressed because the men were talking of stoning him; each one was bitter in spirit because of his sons and daughters. But David found strength in the Lord his God.

1 Samuel 30:1-6

TO SET THE SCENE

A quiz to see how good you are at keeping focused –

1   You have been waiting all week to see a favourite TV programme. Could you enjoy the programme:
- Only if there was absolute silence
- If someone was talking in the same room
- If the children were causing in a riot in the living room

2   You have set aside Friday night as a special time with your spouse/good friend. The phone rings. Would you:
- Ignore it and let it ring

- Put on the answering machine but listen to the message
- Have to pick it up immediately

3 You have an important project to finish at work today but you had a row with your son/daughter before you left the house. Would you:
- Ignore it and get on with your work
- Have it prey on your mind all day
- Ring them up to put the matter straight

Read 1 Samuel 30:1-6

1 David and his fighting men found their homes devastated and their families taken captive. Look back at 1 Samuel 27:1 – why had things started to go wrong for David?

WHAT DOES **2** Scan 1 Samuel 29. David's decision to go into Philistine territory had massive consequences. What difficult situation did **THE BIBLE SAY?** he find himself in?

David's problems culminated in the sacking of Ziklag and the near mutiny of his men. This crisis was a defining moment in his life. In this adversity, David refocused his mind on God and proved to be a great leader.

3 Divide into smaller groups and each group look at a section of 1 Samuel 30:7-31. Discover and then share together all the examples of David's wise leadership.

HOW DOES THIS **4** What impresses you most about David's leadership? What quality of his would you most like to emulate?
APPLY TO ME

5 What was the key that enabled David to turn his crisis situation into a victory? Look at 1 Samuel 30:6.

6 In contrast to David, we read that Saul's 'strength was gone' (1 Sam. 28:20). Why do you think that David and Saul's lives turned out so differently? Perhaps look at 1 Samuel 28:16-19 for ideas.

HOW DOES THIS APPLY TO ME **7** What lessons can we learn from the lives of David and Saul about how to maintain our focus on God even in the difficult times and to live lives that please him?

8 David's obedience and focus on God was only part of the reason for his success. What did God do to help David win the victory? Look at 1 Samuel 30: 11-16.

9 Share examples of similar times when you have seen the divine fingerprint on your life.

WORSHIP
How often have you found your mind wandering in church? Even in our worship times, we find it hard to maintain our focus on God. As you spend time together now in worship – singing songs, praying and praising God – find ways to keep focused. You could light some candles, meditate on a particular verse, kneel if you don't usually kneel to pray, have a picture or image in your mind or even write out your prayers. Be creative!

FOR FURTHER STUDY
Look in your local Christian bookshop for resources on leadership – they are many and varied! Book titles range from *Spiritual Leadership* by O.J. Sanders to *Point Man – How A Man Can Lead His Family* by Steve Farrar.

DURING THE WEEK
Take one practical measure to help keep your focus on God this week. Perhaps set your alarm half an hour earlier so that you can spend time with God, arrange to pray with a friend, or make it a priority to get to the Sunday services.

ACTIVITY PAGE

In 1 Samuel 23:16, Jonathan helped David 'find strength in God' in a moment of crisis. Here in 1 Samuel 30:6, David doesn't have any such support or friendship; even his own fighting men were about to resort to mutiny. He had to 'find strength in God' himself.

It is always good to have Christian friends around us when we face difficulties but at times, like David, we may face our crises alone.

Part of being a disciple-maker is to help people learn to rely on God; to help them turn to him first rather than relying on the faith of others; to teach them how to find strength in God for themselves.

How would you help the people described below to find strength in God for themselves?

▶ Jane has just become a Christian. She has little background in spiritual things but is eager to learn. Her main question is 'What is the best way to read and make sense of the Bible?'

▶ Keith has been a Christian for a while. He's a prominent businessman but struggles with prayer. He asks you ' How do you keep your concentration when you pray, how can you pray for all the needs you know about? My prayers just seem like a shopping list and I never hear God actually speak to me.'

▶ Whenever Sandra's got a problem she rings you up, wanting your advice. What practical ideas could you suggest to her so that she starts relying on God rather than you?

DEALING WITH SUCCESS

AIM: Learning how to keep our focus on God in the good times

We're used to seeing Christian books on 'How to deal with failure', 'How to deal with disappointment' – but rarely do we see books on 'How to deal with success.' When David became king of Judah, the prize of a united kingdom was within his grasp. But what kind of example would he be? Would he keep his feet on the ground and his eyes on God when he became king?

> *All the tribes of Israel came to David at Hebron and said, 'We are your own flesh and blood. In the past, while Saul was king over us, you were the one who led Israel on their military campaigns. And the Lord said to you, 'You shall shepherd my people Israel, and you shall become their ruler.'*
>
> *When all the elders of Israel had come to King David at Hebron, the king made a compact with them at Hebron before the Lord, and they anointed David king over Israel.*
>
> *David was thirty years old when he became king, and he reigned forty years. In Hebron he reigned over Judah seven years and six months, and in Jerusalem he reigned over all Israel and Judah thirty-three years.*
>
> *2 Samuel 5:1-5*

TO SET THE SCENE

Do you find it easier to keep focused on God, to trust and rely on him, when life is going well or when you're going through difficulties? Share your experiences together.

Read 2 Samuel 5:1-5

WHAT DOES SEARCH THE BIBLE SAY?

1 Why did David's power and popularity grow after Saul's death? Split into smaller groups to check out the following references:

- ▶ 2 Samuel 2:4, 3:1-5
- ▶ 2 Samuel 3:6-21
- ▶ 2 Samuel 4:1, 5-8

WHAT DOES SEARCH THE BIBLE SAY?

2 How do we know that David's popularity wasn't down to his own plotting and planning? What is the evidence that David wanted God alone to bring him to the throne? Look at David's response to:

- ▶ The death of Saul and Jonathan – 2 Samuel 1:11-16
- ▶ The death of Abner, commander of the Israelite army – 2 Samuel 3:33-38
- ▶ The death of Ish-Bosheth, king of Israel – 2 Samuel 4:9-12
- ▶ The tribes of Israel – 2 Samuel 5:1-5

3 From chapter 5, what were the key successes of David's reign?

4 Despite these great successes, David hadn't let power go to his head. How do we know this? Look at 2 Samuel 5:11-12, 18-25.

> *The desire to live a God-directed life gets us to the core of David's being.*
>
> **Ian Coffey**

5 What do you consider to be your greatest 'success' in life so far?

6 If God was measuring 'success' in our lives, what do you think he would he look for?

HOW DOES THIS
APPLY TO ME

7 If you're rewarded with secular indicators of success because you've done well in your job – i.e. nice car, good salary etc – what safeguards could you put in place to make sure you keep in line with God's view of success?

8 Consider the following 'success points' in a person's life. At these times, how can we demonstrate our acknowledgement of God's hand on our lives?

▶ Birth of a child
▶ Marriage
▶ Promotion at work
▶ Financial advancement

WORSHIP

In the quietness, bring to God your ambitions and anxieties about work. Share thanksgiving for the 'successes' you have enjoyed, however small they've been. Then read Psalm 27 together, highlighting all the truths about God. And, like David, let your prayers focus on your desire for intimacy with God rather than on your circumstances – whether these are times of success or disappointment. Perhaps play some CDs or tapes to lead you in worship and then pray in twos about your own particular work situation.

FURTHER STUDY

We often think of success in terms of our working life. If you want to investigate work-related issues further, then contact the London Institute for Contemporary Christianity on 0207 399 9555 or www.licc.org.uk. They will provide you with resources and details of other organisations to contact. You might also like to read Mark Greene's *Thank God it's Monday*, and the Spring Harvest books about work-related issues: *More Than a Job* by Jani Rubery, *Exploring Your Vocation* by Matt Bird and Friends, and *Questions of Business Life* by Richard Higginson.

FOR NEXT WEEK

When something good happens to you, what is your immediate response? Do you tell your spouse or a friend – wonder what's around the corner – or feel pleased with yourself for your achievement? This week, get your focus right – practise thanking and praising God when good things happen, before you do anything else.

ACTIVITY PAGE

David had not aggressively promoted himself as king, even when he had the opportunity. How can we get the balance right between letting God bring blessing to us and going out and pursuing it for ourselves?

How would you behave in the following scenarios:

▶ There is an opportunity for promotion at work. Others are interested in the position, so what do you do to promote yourself as the best person for it? What should a Christian's view of ambition be?

▶ You have put an offer in for a house. You prayed and 'put a fleece out' to God saying that if this was the right house for you then the owners would accept your offer. The estate agents ring back to say that the house is yours, if you increase your offer by £3000.

▶ You are already involved in a particular ministry at church. A more senior position in the ministry becomes vacant. Should you tell the church leaders of your interest in this position or believe that if you're the right person for the job, your gifts will be recognised and the leadership will approach you?

LIFE AFTER FAILURE

AIM: To find a way back to God after failure

Elton John was right when he sang 'Sorry seems to be the hardest word'. When we realise the extent of our failure and the mess we've got ourselves, in saying 'sorry' to God seems very painful and at the same time very inadequate. But however hard true repentance is, seeking forgiveness from God is the only way back to him and the only way forward for us.

> *In the spring, at the time when kings go off to war, David sent Joab out with the king's men and the whole Israelite army. They destroyed the Ammonites and besieged Rabbah. But David remained in Jerusalem.*
>
> *One evening David got up from his bed and walked around on the roof of the palace. From the roof he saw a woman bathing. The woman was very beautiful, and David sent someone to find out about her. The man said, 'Isn't this Bathsheba, the daughter of Eliam and the wife of Uriah the Hittite?' Then David sent messengers to get her. She came to him, and he slept with her. (She had purified herself from her uncleanness.) Then she went back home. The woman conceived and sent word to David, saying 'I am pregnant.'*
>
> ***2 Samuel 11:1-5***

TO SET THE SCENE

Failure of varying degrees is common to us all. Brainstorm the names of well-known people who have failed. Think of two categories – secular figures as well as prominent churchmen. Is there any difference between how the two groups handled their failures? How have they coped with life after failure?

Read 2 Samuel 11:1-5

1   Sleeping with Bathsheba wasn't David's first error of judgement. From 2 Samuel 11:1-5, list David's series of mistakes.

2   We fail as Christians in many different ways. What would you say are the key ingredients that lead to failure?

HOW DOES THIS / APPLY TO ME

3   Nathan cleverly helped David realise the extent of his sin (2 Sam. 12:1-14). We're often reticent to point out other people's failings to them – perhaps we're frightened they will return the compliment! But imagine you found out a member of your congregation was involved in serious sin. How would you address the situation, what strategy would you use to help them see their sin if you were a:

> ▶ Church leader?
> ▶ Regular member of the congregation?
> ▶ Close friend?

HOW DOES THIS / APPLY TO ME

4   Check out 2 Samuel 11:6-17 for the spiral of sin that David set in motion to cover up his adultery with Bathsheba. Is your life in a spiral of sin or a spiral of righteousness? What positive measures can we put into our lives so we don't fall into sin but increasingly become more righteous like Jesus?

WHAT DOES / SEARCH / THE BIBLE SAY?

5   Divide into two groups. One group look at Saul's repentance in 1 Samuel 15:1-31 the other group look at David's repentance in Psalm 51:

> ▶ What was wrong with Saul's attempt at repentance?
> ▶ Why was David's repentance acceptable to God?

Godly sorrow brings repentance that leads to salvation and leaves no regret, but worldly sorrow brings death.

2 Corinthians 7:10

6 What does David's example teach us about the way back to God after failure?

 WHAT DOES SEARCH THE BIBLE SAY? **7** David was forgiven by God but still had to live with the consequences of his sin. Look at 2 Samuel 12:10-14 – what were these consequences? How did they unfold in David's life? See 2 Samuel 12:18; 13:28-29; 16: 20-22; 18:15.

8 What is the value of repentance if we still need to live with the consequences of our sin?

9 What have you found to be the best thing about recovering from failure?

WORSHIP
In a time of quietness ask yourself:

- What is stopping me from repenting now?
- Are their areas of my life where I am letting my defences slip and giving room to temptation?
- Am I pursuing God – and all that he has for me – with eagerness?

If it is helpful, you could pray together in twos about some of these issues.

Also pray for:

- Your church and youth group leaders as they counsel those who have failed and are living with the consequences.
- Those whose work or family situations mean they face much temptation i.e. businessmen working away from home.

Then to conclude your prayer time together with a confession:

Father Eternal, giver of light and grace,
we have sinned against you and our fellow men,
in what we have thought,
in what we have said and done,
through ignorance, through weakness
through our own deliberate fault.
We have wounded your love,
and marred your image in us.
We are sorry and ashamed,
and repent of all our sins.
For the sake of your son Jesus Christ, who
died for us,
forgive us all that is past:
and lead us out from darkness
to walk as children of light. Amen

Confession from the Alternative Anglican Service
Book 1980

FOR FURTHER STUDY

Dealing with failure − whether it's personal, a friend's or offering counsel from a church leadership point of view − needs much grace. There are many resources on this topic. A helpful starting place is Philip Yancey's *What's so Amazing About Grace?*

FOR NEXT WEEK

Do three things.

1   Accept God's forgiveness and discipline − remember David only mourned for his child whilst it was alive; after that he accepted God's decision and tried to move on with his life (2 Sam. 12:19-20).

2   Look for evidence of God's grace towards you − amazingly, God gave David and Bathsheba another child and the Bible says 'the Lord loved him' (2 Sam. 12:24).

3   Show God's grace to someone else this week!

FAMILY TIES

AIM: To learn how to live for God in the context of family life

With a murdering son determined to usurp his throne, David must have looked back to his days as a fugitive with fond memories! As with all of us, life had got more complicated and pressurised with increased responsibilities and David was learning the truth of the old adage that 'It's the people we love who hurt us the most.'

> *In the course of time, Absalom provided himself with a chariot and horses and with fifty men to run ahead of him. He would get up early and stand by the side of the road leading to the city gate. Whenever anyone came with a complaint to be placed before the king for a decision, Absalom would call out to him, 'What town are you from?' He would answer, 'Your servant is from one of the tribes of Israel.' Then Absalom would say to him, 'Look, your claims are valid and proper, but there is no representative of the king to hear you.' And Absalom would add, 'If only I were appointed judge in the land! Then everyone who has a complaint or case could come to me and I would see that he receives justice.'*
>
> *Also, whenever anyone approached him to bow down before him, Absalom would reach out his hand, take hold of him and kiss him. Absalom behaved in this way towards all the Israelites who came to the king asking for justice, and so he stole the hearts of the men of Israel.*
>
> ***2 Samuel 15:1-6***

TO SET THE SCENE

We all experience the ups and downs of family life. Have a look at the quiz below to see how you're faring.

How would you describe your family relationships at the moment?

▶ A beautiful day in Barbados – warm and sunny
▶ An August day in Britain – fine with the odd shower
▶ Arctic conditions

What television programme best describes your home life?

- ▶ *The World At War* – you can't do a thing right!
- ▶ *Question Time* – your toddler/teenager is always asking 'why?'
- ▶ *Casualty* – you're tired of dealing with the endless round of coughs and colds
- ▶ *Changing Rooms* – you're at a transition point right now

What song title best describes your family life?

- ▶ Elton John's 'It's no sacrifice' – life's going well, at the moment!
- ▶ Elvis' 'Heartbreak hotel' – your spouse/ children/parents are causing you great angst!
- ▶ John Lennon's 'Imagine' – you're dreaming of a time without nappies/university fees/a wedding to pay for.

Read 2 Samuel 15:1-12

1 What was Absalom's strategy to depose his father as king?

2 Imagine you're trying to improve the relationship between David and Absalom. What would you say to David to encourage him to make up with his son?

Remember:

- ▶ Absalom's sister had been raped (2 Sam. 13: 1-21)
- ▶ Absalom has spent years in exile (2 Sam. 13: 37,38)
- ▶ His popularity was growing (2 Sam. 15:6)

What would you say to Absalom to encourage him to make up with his father?

Remember:

- ▶ He was a murderer (2 Sam. 13:28,29)
- ▶ He was trying to depose his father (2 Sam. 15:1-6)

Unfortunately, events took a turn for the worse: Absalom was crowned king at Hebron and David escaped from Jerusalem. Their troops clashed and Absalom was killed as he fled the scene.

3 How would you apportion blame for this deteriorating father-son relationship?

 HOW DOES THIS **4** Parenting doesn't come with a 'How to' manual and many of us have experienced prodigal children like Absalom. What are APPLY TO ME the most important lessons you've learnt about how to preserve family relationships?

As David looked back over the tragedy, perhaps he realised that the trappings of success and family pressures had lured him into spiritual complacency. Perhaps he looked back longingly to his fugitive days of single-minded devotion to God.

5 In this season of life, what is your number one distraction from devotion to God?

- ▶ Your spouse/friends
- ▶ Difficulty with time management
- ▶ Family responsibilities
- ▶ Work stress
- ▶ Financial concerns
- ▶ Lack of motivation

 WHAT DOES SEARCH THE BIBLE SAY? **6** Nevertheless, with his family in crisis and his closest advisor defecting to Absalom's side, David turned again to God. Look at Psalm 3 and 55:16-23 – what beliefs about God did David have to comfort him?

WHAT DOES SEARCH THE BIBLE SAY?

7 Even in these bleak times, David saw God at work and in control. How is David's faith demonstrated?

Look at:

- ▶ 2 Samuel 15:25
- ▶ 2 Samuel 15:31
- ▶ 2 Samuel 16:5-14

8 In times of family pain, where do you find comfort?

HOW DOES THIS APPLY TO ME?

9 Home is often the hardest place to live as a Christian because our family see what we're really like. What do you would want your spouse/parents/children to learn about God from your life?

WORSHIP

Look back to your answer to question 6. Spend some time worshipping God together for all the truths you read about him in Psalm 3 and 55. Then choose a truth that is particularly precious to you from these Psalms, write it down on a piece of paper and then give it to another person in the group. Let that truth encourage them this week, whatever their circumstances are.

FURTHER STUDY

There are various parenting resources available. For a quick read, there are Rob Parsons' *Sixty Minute Father* and *Sixty Minute Mother*.

FOR NEXT WEEK

Take steps to deal with your number one distraction from devotion to God this week. It might help to share your difficulties and plan of action with a friend, so that they can pray with you and continue to encourage you in the coming weeks.

LEAVING A LEGACY

AIM: To assess the heritage we're leaving for future generations

The financial pundits are puzzled at the current state of the markets; no one is quite sure how to advise potential investors. But whether we like it or not, there's one long-term investment we all make deposits into and that's our legacy. With every action and reaction, we make a daily contribution to our legacy.

David summoned all the officials of Israel to assemble at Jerusalem: the officers over the tribes, the commanders of the divisions in the service of the king, the commanders of thousands and commanders of hundreds, and the officials in charge of all the property and livestock belonging to the king and his sons, together with the palace officials, the mighty men and all the brave warriors.

King David rose to his feet and said: 'Listen to me, my brothers and my people. I had it in my heart to build a house as a place of rest for the ark of the covenant of the Lord, for the footstool of our God, and I made plans to build it. But God said to me, 'You are not to build a house for my Name, because you are a warrior and have shed blood.'

Yet the Lord, the God of Israel chose me from my whole family to be king over Israel for ever. He chose Judah as leader, and from the house of Judah he chose my family, and from my father's sons he was pleased to make me king over all Israel. Of all my sons – and the Lord has given me many – he has chosen my son Solomon to sit on the throne of the kingdom of the Lord over Israel. He said to me: 'Solomon your son is the one who will build my house and my courts, for I have chosen him to be my son, and I will be his father. I will establish his kingdom forever if he is unswerving in carrying out my commands and laws, as is being done at this time.'

1 Chronicles 28:1-7

TO SET THE SCENE

Imagine you're passing on the Olympic torch of faith to the next generation of believers. What sentence would you like inscribed on the torch that would describe your Christian life?

Read 1 Chronicles 28:1-21

1 The construction of the temple was to be the pinnacle of David's legacy but God would not let him build it. Look at 1 Chronicles 28:1-21 – how would you describe David's attitude towards God regarding this issue?

2 To what extent do you share David's attitude, when God doesn't give you what you want?

3 Part of leaving a legacy is planning. What plans had David already made for the temple?

> *David knew what it was to be God-driven and God-directed. He'd learned the difference between a good idea and a God idea.*
>
> ***Ian Coffey***

4 What safeguards can we put in place to ensure our plans are God's ideas rather than just good ideas?

5 Divide into two groups and reflect on David's life – you could scan through 1 Samuel 16 – 2 Samuel 24 if you have time.

▶ One group list all the positive things David did, all the times he was obedient to God.

▶ The other group recall David's failures, the occasions he was disobedient to God.

6 On balance, why do you think David could be described as 'a man after God's own heart'?

> *For when David had served God's purpose in his own generation, he fell asleep; he was buried with his fathers and his body decayed.*
>
> ***Acts 13:36***

7 What lessons have you learnt from the life of David?

8 As you seek to be a person after God's own heart, think about the legacy you're leaving.

Think through:
- How would your best friend/spouse describe your Christian commitment?
- What are your children learning about living as a Christian from you?
- Having worked with you, what would your colleagues' view of Christianity be?
- Are you happy with your level of devotion to God?
- What impressions do church folk/neighbours have of you?

Now think through all these areas again:
- What legacy would I like to leave?
- What things need to change so that from a Christian point of view I can be satisfied with the legacy I leave?

WORSHIP

Our Christian life is like any other investment – if we want significant returns we need to make substantial deposits. Sacrifice has always been part of the life of faith. The temple, where many sacrifices were offered, was built on the site of Mount Moriah, the place Abraham was going to sacrifice Isaac. It was also built on the threshing floor David had bought to make a sacrifice to the Lord to stop the plague (2 Sam. 24). He said to the owner of the land 'I insist on paying for it. I will not sacrifice to the Lord my God burnt offerings that cost me nothing.'

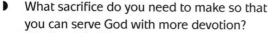

- ▶ What sacrifice do you need to make so that you can serve God with more devotion?
- ▶ What do you need to give up so that God can have more of your heart?
- ▶ In a time of quiet, offer your sacrifice to God

As you make your commitments to God, remember that nearby the site of the temple, just outside Jerusalem's city walls, Jesus made the ultimate sacrifice for us. Share communion together as you reflect on his sacrifice.

FOR FUTURE WEEKS

Write the letter described on the Activity Page and start putting practices in place that will help you leave a legacy you and God will be pleased with.

ACTIVITY PAGE

On some notepaper write a letter to yourself. Write down your thoughts from your answers to question 8 – describe the legacy you'd like to leave and the changes needed to make this happen.

With God's help start taking action today – remember your legacy is a daily investment!

At turning points in your life – when you need to make an important decision, you're struggling with family life, or when failure comes – look at the letter to remind you of your key values and the legacy you want to leave.

Remember God also invests in the legacy of those whose hearts are devoted to him:

He chose David his servant
and took him from the sheep pens;
from tending sheep he brought him
to be the shepherd of his people Jacob,
of Israel his inheritance.
And David shepherded them with
integrity of heart;
with skilful hands he led them.

Psalm 78:70-72

LEADERS' GUIDE

TO HELP YOU LEAD

You may have led a housegroup many times before or this may be your first time. Here is some advice on how to lead these studies:

▶ As a group leader, you don't have to be an expert or a lecturer. You are there to facilitate the learning of the group members − helping them to discover for themselves the wisdom in God's word. You should not be doing most of the talking or dishing out the answers, whatever the group expects from you!

▶ You do need to be aware of the group's dynamics, however. People can be quite quick to label themselves and each other in a group situation. One person might be seen as the expert, another the moaner who always has something to complain about. One person may be labelled as quiet and not be expected to contribute; another person may always jump in with something to say. Be aware of the different type of individuals in the group, but don't allow the labels to stick. You may need to encourage those who find it hard to get a word in, and quieten down those who always have something to say. Talk to members between sessions to find out how they feel about the group.

▶ The sessions are planned to try and engage every member in active learning. Of course you cannot force anyone to take part if they don't want to, but it won't be too easy to be a spectator. Activities that ask everyone to write down a word, or talk in twos, and then report back to the group are there for a reason. They give everyone space to think and form their opinion, even if not everyone voices it out loud.

▶ Do adapt the sessions for your group as you feel is appropriate. Some groups may know each other very well and will be prepared to talk at a deep level. New groups may take a bit of time to get to know each other before making themselves vulnerable, but encourage members to share their lives with each other.

▶ You probably won't be able to tackle all the questions in each session so decide in advance which ones are most appropriate to your group and situation.

▶ Encourage a number of replies to each question. The study is not about finding a single right answer, but about sharing experiences and thoughts in order to find out how to apply the Bible to people's lives. When brainstorming, don't be too quick to evaluate the contributions. Write everything down and then have a look to see which suggestions are worth keeping.

▶ Similarly, encourage everyone to ask questions, to voice doubts and to discuss difficulties. Some parts of the Bible are difficult to understand. Sometimes the Christian faith throws up paradoxes. Painful things happen to us that make it difficult to see what God is doing. A housegroup should be a safe place to express all of this. If discussion doesn't resolve the issue, send everyone away to pray about it between sessions, and ask your minister for advice.

▶ Give yourself time in the week to read through the Bible passage and the questions. Read the Leaders' notes for the session, as different ways of presenting the questions are sometimes suggested. However, during the session, don't be too quick to come in with the answer – sometimes people need space to think.

▶ Delegate as much as you like! The easiest activities to delegate are reading the text and the worship sessions, but there are other ways to involve the group members. Giving people responsibility can help them own the session much more.

▶ Pray for group members by name, that God would meet with them during the week. Pray for the group session, for a constructive and helpful time. Ask the Lord to equip you as you lead the group.

THE STRUCTURE OF EACH SESSION

Feedback: find out what people remember from the previous session, or if they have been able to act during the week on what was discussed last time.

To set the scene: an activity or a question to get everyone thinking about the subject to be studied.

Bible reading: it's important actually to read the passage you are studying during the session. Ask someone to prepare this in advance or go around the group reading a verse or two each. Don't assume everyone will be happy to read out loud.

Questions and activities: adapt these as appropriate to your group. Some groups may enjoy a more activity-based approach; some may prefer just to discuss the questions. Try out some new things!

Worship: suggestions for creative worship and prayer are included, which give everyone an opportunity to respond to God, largely individually. Use these alongside singing or other group expressions of worship. Add a prayer time with opportunities to pray for group members and their families and friends.

For next week: this gives a specific task to do during the week, helping people to continue to think about or apply what they have learned.

For further study: suggestions are given for those people who want to study the themes further. These could be included in the housegroup if you feel it's appropriate and if there is time.

WHAT YOU NEED
A list of materials that are needed is printed at the start of each session in the Leaders' Guide. In addition you will probably need:

Bibles: the main Bible passage is printed in the book so that all the members can work from the same version. It would be useful to have other Bibles available, or to ask everyone to bring their own, so that other passages can be referred to.

Paper and Pens: for people who need more space than is in the book!

Flip chart: it is helpful to write down people's comments during a brainstorming session, so that none of the suggestions is lost. They may not be space for a proper flip chart in the average lounge, and having one may make it feel too much like a business meeting or lecture. Try getting someone to write on a big sheet of paper on the floor or coffee table, and then stick this up on the wall with blu-tack.

GROUND RULES
How do people know what is expected of them in a housegroup situation? Is it ever discussed, or do we just pick up clues from each other? You may find it helpful to discuss some ground rules for the housegroup at the start of this course, even if your group has been going a long time. This also gives you an opportunity to talk about how you, as the leader, see the group. Ask everyone to think about what they want to get out of the course. How do they want the group to work? What values do they want to be part of the group's experience; honesty, respect, confidentiality? How do they want their contributions to be treated? You could ask everyone to write down three ground rules on slips of paper and put them in a bowl. Pass the bowl around the group. Each person takes out a rule and reads it, and someone collates the list. Discuss the ground rules that have been suggested and come up with a top five. This method enables everyone to contribute fairly anonymously. Alternatively, if your group are all quite vocal, have a straight discussion about it!

NB Not all questions in each session are covered, some are self-explanatory.

ICONS

 The aim of the session

 Engaging with the world

 Investigate what else the Bible says

 How does this apply to me?

 What about my church?

www.springharvest.org/workbooks/

SESSION 1

MATERIALS NEEDED

Flip chart, pens and paper

CDs or tapes and a music system if you think it would be helpful for the worship session

TO SET THE SCENE

If this is the first time your group has met together, then take time to introduce each other. Sharing big decisions you have had to make will be a good way to learn about each other and your backgrounds. As others share their experiences of God's guidance, they may be very different from your own, but see what you can learn from them.

1   Samuel was a prophet and chief advisor to king Saul. It would have caused quite a stir for such a significant figure to come to Bethlehem.

2   Saul did not wait for Samuel to come and offer sacrifices – he thought he could act independently of God's law and his prophet. Also he didn't obey God's instruction to destroy all the Amalekites and their possessions. He put his own will above God's and when he was caught, he tried to justify himself.

3   The people ask for a king, despite God's warnings of what he would be like, because they wanted to be like the other nations. God had nothing against kingship (Deut. 17:14-20) but the tone of the request showed that the Israelites were rejecting God. This king was to replace God and so the whole venture was soured from the start.

4   Samuel was still mourning over Saul's disobedience and the fact that God had rejected him. He was looking back to the past and thinking about what could have been. We do the same thing. Often we're not aware of where God is working because we have our own fixed ideas and expectations of what he should be doing.

5   To test if something is in God's will we need to: search the Scriptures, pray, seek counsel from godly Christians, sense God's peace in our hearts, and test the opportunities.

6   [b] We often label people in our churches – some are in the charismatic wing, others in the trendy crowd, others 'in' with the minister etc. Seeing people as God sees them involves the daily renewal of our minds (Rom. 12:2). But it helps if we take people on face value rather than listening to others' perceptions of them; if we pray for them and their ministry and if we try to appreciate their backgrounds and the influences that have shaped them.

7   Perhaps God would see that the time we spend with our children is more influential than we realise, that how we treat our secretary is more important than the clients we try to win and that the letters we write to the Prime Minister or television companies expressing a Christian worldview are worthwhile – who knows! As you analyse your own situation, think of practical ways you can reflect God's value system in your everyday life.

8   Come up with as many lessons David would have to learn as you can: for example, waiting on God's timing, praise and worship in the midst of hardship, the value of true friendship, acknowledging God's hand behind his victories and appreciating God as his strength and protection.

SESSION 2

MATERIALS NEEDED

CDs or tapes and a music system if you think it would be helpful for the worship session

TO SET THE SCENE

Don't let people feel awkward if they say they haven't got a 'best friend' – encourage them to think back to good friendships from school or childhood. This exercise is to set people thinking about what makes a good friendship and what makes us 'click' with some people and not others.

1   You may be surprised at some of the answers to this question! There'll be characteristics both groups share such as faithfulness, trust, and reliability. Perhaps for women, such issues as time, relationship building, sharing, similar age and stage of life might be more significant factors than for men. For men perhaps common tasks cultivate their friendships. If big issues are thrown up by this question relating to people's difficulties in making friends, be sensitive and, if necessary, follow up individuals later.

2   David – trusted Jonathan, grieved bitterly over his death and looked after his son, Mephibosheth. Jonathan – warned David of trouble, protected him from Saul, spoke well of him to his father, had a generous spirit (1 Sam 20:4), and had genuine self-giving love (1 Sam 20:17). Both men were committed to each other.

3   Jonathan accepted David as his equal and gave him the symbols of royal status. He was humble, generous and committed to their friendship, despite the fact that David was taking his role and inheritance.

4   Jonathan could have reacted like his father and tried to protect his own position. He could have been jealous of David's military prowess and his popular appeal.

6   Perhaps they prayed, read the Scriptures, sang Psalms, and mediated together. Or perhaps Jonathan just listened to David and then helped him gain a proper perspective of God again.

7   It would be helpful if we all had at least one relationship where we could talk about spiritual things, encourage each other in our daily devotional lives, and pray together.

8 Moses had an intimacy with God, Abraham was God's friend because he trusted and believed him, and we can be Jesus' friends if we obey his commands.

9 Come up with practical suggestions for improving your friendship with God – e.g. spend more time with him, read his word, listen to him, trust him, obey him. Use your answers to questions 5 and 8 to give you some ideas.

SESSION 3

MATERIALS NEEDED

A range of up-to-date newspapers

Paper and pens, drawing pins/nails, notice board or wooden cross, CDs or tapes and music system for worship section

TO SET THE SCENE

Often the enemies of Christianity are subtle and their message insidious; they appear harmless e.g. horoscopes or materialism - the pressure from advertising and commerce to be the same as everyone else in our lifestyles, ambitions and spending patterns. Other threats such as Islamic terrorists seem much more blatant. Our enemies vary in their level of opposition and threat. Nevertheless, however dangerous they are, we seem to have an enormous capacity to ignore them and get on with everyday life!

1 Saul was jealous of David's popularity and his military prowess. The evil spirit exacerbated his feelings of inadequacy and made him fearful because God's spirit was on David.

2 Saul made six attempts on David's life – three times with a spear, twice by luring him to attack the Philistines by offering his daughters as prizes, once by sending a squad to his home. After this, there was an all-out hunt for David.

3 Psalm 59 – given his circumstances David surprisingly speaks three times of God's love and strength and asks God not to kill his enemies. Psalm 23 – he talks about God looking after his well-being, giving him security and making him flourish. Despite his circumstances, he regards God's goodness and love towards him as lavish.

4 David refuses to kill Saul because he was the Lord's anointed – God had brought Saul to prominence and it was God's prerogative alone to remove him from office. David wanted to leave room for God to take decisive action against Saul rather than interfere himself.

5 David's example teaches us a number of lessons: David recognised God was at work and so was patient; he continued showing respect to Saul; he continued to make right, God-honouring choices despite the behaviour of Saul; he trusted God to fulfil his promises rather than taking matters into his own hands; he fled from an enemy that threatened to overwhelm him.

www.springharvest.org/workbooks/

6   We need to stay obedient to God and his particular plan for us rather than looking around at everyone else's prosperity etc. We need to be disciplined in our conversation and thought-life so that bitterness does not spread. We should practise being joyful for others when they are successful.

7   This is a personal question – we're usually hurt most by the people we love most, whether or not they are Christians. Share ideas of how to deal with emotional hurt so as not to let it destroy you.

8   Opposition has been part of Christian experience from the very early days. We prove the genuineness of our faith by persevering through trials, and it is a means of purifying us ready for heaven.

WORSHIP

This can be a very effective exercise. Create a worshipful atmosphere by playing some CDs or tapes. If you can have a cross for people to pin their pieces of paper on then that is the best, if not a notice board would do. Assure people that their notes will be kept confidential and destroyed after the evening.

SESSION 4

MATERIALS NEEDED

Flip chart, paper and pens

Tapes or CDs, a music system, candles, pictures or images – whatever you would find helpful for the worship time

TO SET THE SCENE

This exercise is designed to be a fun quiz. We all operate differently – some people are more easily distracted than others, some are able to focus more on people, others on tasks. But however we're wired, with the Holy Spirit's help, we're all able to focus on Jesus.

1   David took his eyes off God and took matters into his own hands. Instead of trusting God for his security, he used his own logic and fled to Philistine territory.

2   David finds himself facing a moral dilemma – having to fight on behalf of the Philistines against his own people, the Israelites. It was only because the Philistine commanders objected to his presence that David was released from this task.

3   He sought God's will before he took action, he obeyed what God told him to do, he showed compassion to the weak, he acknowledged his victory was due to the Lord, he respected the roles of each of his men equally, and he gave an offering back to God.

5   David refocused his mind and actions on God. In the midst of the crisis, he found his strength in God.

6   David's repentance was heartfelt, he sought God, and he relied on God's resources. Saul did not obey God or repent sincerely when he was found out. To him, the worship of God was a convenience rather than a commitment. He relied on his own resources and they ran out.

7   Continual turning to God is the only course of action for us if we want to stay focused on him. We need to learn to rely on his strength, power and protection alone. We should not allow failures to destroy us but rather repent and move on in obedience. Neither should we listen to negative influences.

8 God allowed David's men to find an Egyptian slave who had been part of the raid

in Ziklag. He was able to show them exactly where the Amalekites were so that David could recover everything – the plunder and the families.

SESSION 5

MATERIALS NEEDED

Flip chart, pens and paper

CDs, tapes and music system for the worship section

TO SET THE SCENE

Encourage people to share their stories. We are usually more prone to turning to God when we are at the end of our own resources rather than when things are going well. Dealing with success isn't a topic that is often dealt with and we need to discover ways to keep our focus on God in these times.

1 David became king of Judah; his family grew more influential as he married wives from different areas and had many children; Abner, the commander of the Israelite army defected and promised to bring the tribes of Israel under his rule; Ish-Bosheth, the king of Israel, and the tribes ruled by him were overawed by David's power; Ish-Bosheth was murdered, leaving the way open for David to become king.

2 David did not welcome any aggressive means to make him king. For example, he was not pleased when Saul, Jonathan, or Ish-Bosheth were killed, even though they were obstacles to his coming to the throne. Although Abner had defected, he was still perceived by many as dangerous, yet David mourned his death. David waited for the elders to come to him to make him king.

3 He conquered Jerusalem – the city on the border between the two parts of his realm and so unified the territory without having to subordinate one region to the other. He defeated Israel's chief enemy, the Philistines.

4 David knew that he hadn't achieved this prominence of his own accord but that God had done it for him – and not just for him but for the nation of Israel and his plan of redemption. Also, David didn't take action against his enemies without consulting God and then was obedient.

5 Affirm everyone's contribution, whether or not they feel they have enjoyed 'success' in their lives.

6 Of all David's accolades, the chief is that he was a man 'after God's own heart'. This too, is success for us. As Paul said, the goal is 'to know Christ'. The markers for this are a life of integrity, an intimate knowledge of the Scriptures, a vibrant prayer life, an interest in seeing others come to the Lord, a love for God's people and being a discipleship maker.

7 Come up with as many ideas as possible. You could have an accountability/ mentoring relationship with a mature Christian, sharing with them the temptations and stresses you face. You could pray with someone at the high-stress points, such as tax return time for accountants or OFSTED time for teachers. You could be disciplined in your giving to God's work rather than just improving your lifestyle, as your contemporaries will be doing.

8 We can acknowledge God's hand in these things; for example, a thanksgiving service for a child's birth; the style, content and tone of a marriage service; publicly thanking God for promotion in a small group setting; increasing our giving to God's work by supporting a missionary etc. Encourage your group to come up with as many practical ideas as possible.

SESSION 6

LEADERS' GUIDE

Be sensitive when dealing with this issue as it will affect everyone in different ways. Your group members may not share David's experience but each will have had or will have experience of trying to find their way back to God after failure and living with the consequences of their sin. It's probably not appropriate to share major failures in a group context but you may want to follow up with people during the week.

MATERIALS NEEDED
Flip chart, pens and paper

TO SET THE SCENE
All of us have failed and prominent people deal with failure in the same ways that we do − by covering it up, by 'spin', further lying, false repentance; or by humble acknowledgement of their wrongful actions. Perhaps the believers who have truly repented and faced their situation with honesty before God and others like David did are the ones that God can use again in his service.

1   He was complacent and didn't go out to war as he should have done (v1), he continued to look at Bathsheba whilst she was bathing (v2), he sent someone to find out about her (v3), knowing she was someone else's wife, he still sent for her and when she came, he completely gave into his lustful desires and slept with her (v4).

2   Acting in our own power and strength rather than acknowledging God (notice all the 'David sent' verbs in 2 Samuel 11 − he'd forgotten that he was a man 'sent' by God, the power had gone to his head); giving in to temptation and compromise; becoming spiritually complacent; and thinking that no one will find out.

3   As a church leader − use the principles from Matthew 18:15-20 and 1 Corinthians 5 − if the individual consistently refuses to admit their sin, then expose their wrongdoing to the church and treat them as a stranger. But always leave the way back for restoration. As a church member and friend, confront the person privately, and then, if they don't respond, let the church leaders deal with it. As a friend this is difficult to do, but remember the aim is to bring the individual back to God.

4   Maintain your devotional life and your contacts with Christian fellowship, have an accountability relationship with another Christian and an attitude of thanksgiving and acknowledgement of God's sovereignty.

5   Saul was sorry he'd been caught rather than sorry for what he's done; he blamed others for his actions; he claimed pious intentions; he tried to justify himself; and despite his sin he wanted to present himself in a positive light to the people. David pleaded for God's mercy; he recognised the offence of his sin before God rather than trying to justify himself; he knew his sin was part of who he was and what he'd become rather than a one-off act; he humbly asked God for cleansing; and he wanted God's forgiveness rather than human approval.

6   Forgiveness and a restored relationship with God are possible if we are sincere in our repentance, if we appreciate the seriousness of our offence before God and are no longer interested in preserving our dignity at the expense of God's glory.

7   There would be violence and disaster in his household; a close relative would shame him publicly by sleeping with his wives; and his son would die. All this came true – Solomon died; his son Absalom murdered his other son Amnon; Absalom himself was killed after he slept with his father's concubines.

8   We are now back in God's will; we have the joy of a restored relationship with him (Ps. 51); we have the Holy Spirit's strength to deal with the consequences of our sin; and we can even see God's graciousness in our life.

SESSION 7

MATERIALS NEEDED
Flip chart, pens and paper

CD or tapes and music system if you'd find it helpful in the worship session

TO SET THE SCENE
Family issues can cause great sadness and hurt. This icebreaker is designed to focus people on the theme without it being too painful for them. From people's answers, you'll be able to gauge their general situation and can decide whether some need following up on an one-to-one basis later.

1   Absalom's strategy was to appear powerful with his chariot and security guards; to promise greater justice when he came to power; to stroke people's egos, and to become more popular than his father was so that his usurpation of the throne would meet with the people's support or at least their acquiescence.

2   You could point out to David why Absalom would feel hurt –David hadn't avenged Tamar's rape; he'd ostracised Absalom even when he'd returned from exile; David seemed out of touch and uninterested in what was going on in the country. You could encourage David that Absalom needed a father; he needed someone to challenge him and put his energy to good use. You could point out to Absalom that it was unsurprising his father was distant, given Absalom's actions against Amnon. Instead of working against his father to seize the throne Absalom needed to get rid of his own bitterness and prove his loyalty. Perhaps you could remind Absalom that David's own moral failings might have clouded his judgement when he was dealing with Amnon.

3   There was blame on both sides. David had relinquished his responsibilities as a father and seemed unwilling to intervene in his son's strategy to usurp power until crisis struck. Absalom had tried to take revenge for his sister's rape into his own hands. His own bitterness led to this elaborate take-over bid.

4   Come up with as many suggestions as you can – for example, keeping the lines of communication open, having meals together, creating opportunities for special times together.

5   Encourage people to be honest here.

6 Psalm 3 – God was his shield, he honoured him, was his protector, answered his prayers, sustained him, removed fear, was a deliverer and poured out blessings on him. Psalm 55 – God was his salvation, he heard him, was his protection, his sustainer, would bring about justice, and was trustworthy.

7 2 Samuel 15:25 – rather then use the Ark of the Covenant as a superstitious talisman David sent it back to Jerusalem, knowing that only God could restore him to the throne. 2 Samuel 15:31 – he prayed when his trusted advisor defected to Absalom's side. 2 Samuel 16:5-14 – he believed the possibility that God might be speaking to him even through Shimei's curses.

SESSION 8

MATERIALS NEEDED

Flip chart, pens and paper

CD or tapes and music system if it would be helpful for worship

Bread and wine if you're going to share communion together

TO SET THE SCENE

This exercise is to help people start thinking about the Christian legacy they are passing on to the future generation. As your group thinks what it would like to have inscribed on the torch – 'Faithful to the end', 'Served God fully', or 'Thankful in all things' – they might start to think what may actually be inscribed. This will prepare them to reflect on the changes they need to make so that their legacy is God-honouring.

1   David did not seem to dwell on his personal disappointment but accepted God's will in the matter. He recognised God's sovereignty throughout his life, that God had chosen him for certain tasks and not others (v4-7). He continued to be wholehearted in his devotion to God and urged his son to be the same (v9). He wasn't bitter but was willing to play his part – receiving the plans from God to facilitate his son's building project (v11-19). Despite being rejected as the builder, David still trusted in God's faithfulness (v20).

2   We often take a long time to get over our disappointment and bitterness. We're quick to question the goodness and sovereignty of God when life doesn't turn out as we'd anticipated. It takes a lot of graciousness to facilitate the next generation for a great work for God that we ultimately will not be a part of.

3   He had made plans for the building; had organised arrangements for the priests and Levites; and determined the weight of the gold and silver to be used for the ceremonial temple tools.

4   We should be sensitive to God's Spirit, praying though ideas, asking for confirmation, offering any plans to him and being willing for him to shut the door on them or to present new opportunities to us. We should test whether God is working in a particular area and seek advice from godly leaders. If it's God's idea rather than our own we'll be willing to involve others, let them run with it, rather than holding on to it selfishly so we receive the glory.

5   Positive aspects of David's life: he killed Goliath in God's strength; he never attacked Saul or any other claimants to the throne, trusting God would make him king in his time; he was a good friend to Jonathan and looked after his crippled son; he was a brave soldier and loyal to his fighting men; he knew how to find strength in God and humbly turned to him for help on occasions such as after the devastation of Ziklag; initially he didn't let power go to his head but was a wise king – making Jerusalem the capital, defeating the Philistines etc; he graciously accepted he wasn't to build the temple; his life and prayers were characterised by thanksgiving to God, he readily acknowledged God's hand in his life; and he was always quick and sincere in his repentance, e.g. after counting his fighting men.

Negative aspects of David's life: he went to live in Philistine territory and joined their army to keep safe rather than trusting God's protection; he committed adultery with Bathsheba and murdered her husband Uriah; he did not avenge his daughter's rape; he didn't welcome Absalom back after his exile; he seemed to become complacent and didn't take action against Absalom as he accumulated power ready for the coup; and in a moment of pride he counted his fighting men.

6   David's life was full of faithful obedience but at the same time he lapsed into serious sin. Perhaps he was described as 'a man after God's own heart' because he knew how to repent, he was sincere in his desire for God, he was overwhelmed by God's goodness rather than demanding it; he was willing to let God be God and never sought to usurp God's power or authority. Discuss your ideas together as a group.

WORSHIP
If you're planning to share communion together, it might be appropriate to ask your minister/leaders for their agreement.

FOR FURTHER READING

The life of David brings up many issues that you might like to look at further. An ideal book for further reading is Ian Coffey's *The Story of David*, published by Spring Harvest, which provides many of the themes for this workbook. Here is a list of other books to help you study further:

Leap over a Wall – Eugene Peterson
The Bible Speaks Today – Psalms – Michael Wilcock
The Story of David: After God's own Heart – Ian Coffey
Desiring God – John Piper
What's so Amazing about Grace? – Philip Yancey
A Passion for Holiness – J.I. Packer
The Call – Os Guinness
Spiritual Leadership – O.J. Sanders
Point Man – How a man can lead his family – Steve Farrar
Thank God it's Monday – Mark Greene
More Than a Job – Jani Rubery
Exploring Your Vocation – Matt Bird and Friends
Questions of Business Life – Richard Higginson
Sixty Minute Father – Rob Parsons
Sixty Minute Mother – Rob Parsons

NOTES

NOTES